R00311 66596

CHICAGO PUBLIC LIBRARY
HAROLD WASHINGTON LIBRARY CENTER

R0031166596

REF.
LB
2829
.R57   Rising costs in
       education

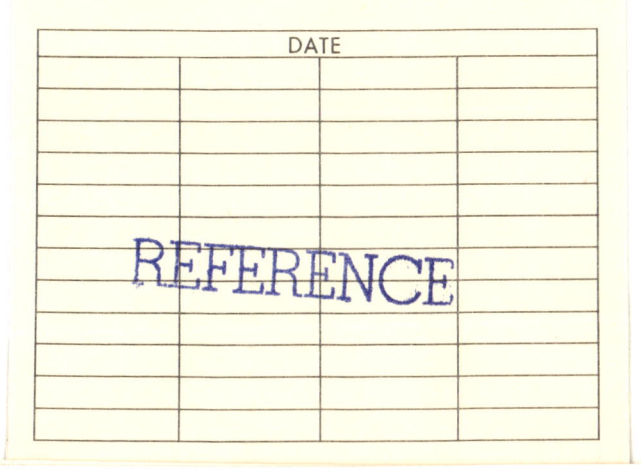

| DATE | | | |
|---|---|---|---|
| | | | |
| | | | |
| | | | |
| | | | |
| | REFERENCE | | |
| | | | |
| | | | |
| | | | |

FORM 125 M

Cop.1 SOCIAL SCIENCES AND HISTORY DIVISION

The Chicago Public Library

Received  MAR 3 1980

EDUCATION & PHILOSOPHY

FORM 125 M

# RISING COSTS IN EDUCATION: THE FEDERAL RESPONSE?

John Charles Daly, *Moderator*

Ernest L. Boyer
Bob Packwood
John Ryor
Thomas Sowell

A Round Table held on March 20, 1978
and sponsored by
the American Enterprise Institute
for Public Policy Research
Washington, D.C.

This pamphlet contains the edited transcript of
one of a series of AEI forums.
These forums offer a medium for
informal exchanges of ideas on current policy problems
of national and international import.
As part of AEI's program of providing opportunities
for the presentation of competing views,
they serve to enhance the prospect
that decisions within our democracy will be based
on a more informed public opinion.
AEI forums are also available on
audio and color-video cassettes.

AEI Forum 17

© 1978 by American Enterprise Institute
for Public Policy Research, Washington, D.C.
Permission to quote from
or reproduce materials in this publication is granted
when due acknowledgment is made.

ISBN 0-8447-2128-X
Library of Congress Catalog Card No. 78-60448

*Printed in United States of America*

JOHN CHARLES DALY, former ABC news executive and forum moderator: The subject of this Public Policy Forum, part of a series presented by the American Enterprise Institute, is Rising Costs in Education: The Federal Response.

In the opening weeks of 1978, a Senate Human Resources Committee bill known as the Pell bill (S. 2539) went to the Senate. It was described on its title page as legislation for the amendment of the basic educational opportunity grants program and for other purposes. The other purposes, it is fair to say, included sidetracking Senate Finance Committee legislation, the Packwood-Moynihan bill, which proposes tax credits for all tuition payments.

The Pell bill, which is very similar in content to President Carter's proposals, would give middle-income families eligibility for benefits under the current scholarship, work-study, and other grant and loan programs.

The Finance Committee's Packwood-Moynihan bill, on the other hand, would allow the taxpayer to take a credit of 50 percent of his tuition and fees. At the outset, that credit would be limited to $250 and would be confined to college students. Two years after the bill's enactment, the tax credit would increase to a maximum of $500, and it would extend to elementary and secondary students, and eventually to graduate students as well.

The battle lines on educational tax credits and relief for

the costs of private elementary and secondary education are not newly drawn. In the past ten years, six tax credit proposals for college expenses have passed the U.S. Senate, only to fail in the House. As early as 1972, well over 100 bills for nonpublic elementary and secondary school tax credits were pending in the House. But all have fallen by the wayside.

Now the hour of decision has arrived. A tax credit opponent and cosponsor of the Pell bill, Senator Javits of New York, has declared that the public feeling on this subject is very serious, and that either the Pell or the Packwood-Moynihan bill is bound to clear the Congress in 1978.

Hanging like the sword of Damocles over all programs to provide federal help to private education, especially to parochial schools, is the First Amendment question of the separation of church and state. With a decision pending in the House on the two education bills, Attorney General Griffin Bell announced that he believes the Supreme Court would rule unconstitutional a bill to provide tax credits. The Packwood-Moynihan bill anticipated the raising of this issue. It provides that if the constitutional question is brought to a U.S. district court, the court shall immediately defer the question to the U.S. court of appeals for that circuit. The court of appeals shall hear the matter with all judges sitting. Any appeal from its decision must be brought to the Supreme Court within twenty days after the court of appeals has ruled. These measures are meant to expedite a test of the bill's constitutionality.

That is the general picture. Senator Packwood, what moved your committee to propose federal income tax credits for education expenses?

BOB PACKWOOD, United States senator (Republican, Oregon): Mr. Daly, there was a 14-to-1 vote in the committee on a bill that fifty-one senators sponsored. We were looking for a simple, equitable way to give a tax break to the person who is putting himself through school, or sending his child through school.

The bill calls for a simple 50 percent tax credit. If a person is paying $400 per year for tuition, he takes $200 off his income tax. That is the sum and substance of the bill. The overwhelming bulk of the support goes to the middle-income taxpayers. It is a simple, honest, equitable way to aid people who are burdened by educational costs.

MR. DALY: Commissioner Boyer, the administration opposes the Packwood-Moynihan bill. Why does it favor the Pell bill's expanded benefits program instead?

ERNEST L. BOYER, United States commissioner of education: We continue to support the notion that federal aid to education should be related to need. We do not think it reasonable to propose the same amount of aid to one family that earns $5,000 and another that earns $50,000. With limited resources, it is important to target aid on the basis of need. We cannot justify an across-the-board grant that would be unusually costly and that would not greatly benefit people.

Clearly, we need a balanced program that would continue the present arrangement: providing grants for the low-income, grants plus work-study programs for the middle-income, and government-subsidized loans for the high-income. This arrangement represents the best use of federal money in relation to family and student need.

MR. DALY: In your opinion, Professor Sowell, what would be the effect of these two proposals on the quality of education?

THOMAS SOWELL, professor of economics, University of California at Los Angeles: The Packwood-Moynihan bill is a revolutionary concept in American education. If this bill were passed, low- to middle-income people could, for the first time, choose their children's schools. They would no longer be at the mercy of those who control the local school monopoly.

The Pell bill is business as usual. It provides grants-in-aid to colleges. Yet, the need is greatest at the elementary and secondary levels, especially for low-income people. If their children get off to a bad start in elementary and secondary school, very little can be done at the college level, despite a great deal of rhetoric to the contrary.

It comes down to a question of choice and power. Will the parent choose his child's school, or will the educational establishment maintain the power to control the funds and thereby call the tune?

MR. DALY: Mr. Ryor, why does the National Education Association support the Pell bill and oppose the Packwood-Moynihan bill?

JOHN RYOR, president, National Education Association: Two issues are involved. The first, of course, is the right of parents to send their children to private schools, if they so choose. And the second is whether or not the public legislative bodies have any responsibility for funding that choice.

Senator Pell's proposal does a better job of giving relief than the tax credit proposal made by Senators Packwood and Moynihan. An additional $250 million in basic grants would benefit some 2.8 million more students. In the work-study program, 80 percent of student-earned wages would be paid by government grants. The guaranteed student loans would add $327 million more to the current $540 million in the program. The limit on family income would be extended to $45,000, making it possible for more middle-income families to benefit from those loan programs.

MR. DALY: There does seem to be basic disagreement as to the ends which would be achieved by these two possible approaches.

SENATOR PACKWOOD: The disagreement is not about ends, but about method.

MR. DALY: All right, let us examine the two methods more closely.

It has been said that the Packwood-Moynihan bill would assist persons who do not need help. Senator Packwood, do you feel that your bill would do that?

SENATOR PACKWOOD: We can accomplish as much with a tax credit as we can accomplish with a grant. We can decide that no one who earns more than $25,000 can have a tax credit. The administration's grant approach, where people fill out forms, apply to the government, and get some money, is limited to incomes of $25,000 or less. Our proposal can do the same thing.

We can alter our approach depending on whom we want to help. The real issue, though, is philosophy. Do we want a system whereby the taxpayer is free to choose, and, depending on his choice, he can make a simple subtraction from his income tax? Nobody in the Department of Health, Education, and Welfare or at the college of his choice needs to be involved. The decision is made by the parent and his child or by part-time students putting themselves through school.

Why should we go through the process of sending application forms to the university and then to HEW? I have a form here called the Basic Educational Opportunity Grant form. It looks something like the income tax form. This is the administration's idea of simplicity. [Laughter.]

There are sections dealing with nontaxable income,

social security, child support, welfare, and so on. And it asks people to state their total federal income tax as it appears on line 20, IRS Form 1040, or line 19, 1040A. This should not be a test for funds. It should be a test for application to college. [Laughter.]

Frankly, much of the information sought in this form is not the government's business, such as how much one's parents make, or what kind of property they own, or how much they received from rents last year. I think our system is simpler, and it can apply to the same income group as the administration's program does.

The administration and HEW object to the Packwood-Moynihan proposal because it would cause them to lose control. They don't like that. They would rather keep control with the Pell bill.

COMMISSIONER BOYER: Senator Packwood, keeping control is not my objective. If I felt that the proposal you have set forth would, in fact, be good public policy, I would be the first to endorse it.

You have pointed out that the Basic Grant form is complex. I believe it is a mistake to change public policy just because a form is complicated. Just last weekend I was working on my income tax, which is much more complex than the form you object to.

You have suggested that the proposed tax relief need not apply across-the-board; that, in fact, it might be tailored to a variety of circumstances. But I might point out that the Senate Finance Committee has greatly complicated the income tax form in order to tailor *it* to a variety of circumstances. Thus, it is hard to avoid detailed forms, and that is not the issue at stake here, anyway. The issue is whether or not there will be relief independent of need.

SENATOR PACKWOOD: No, that is not the issue.

COMMISSIONER BOYER: It seems more central to me than whether or not a given form is complicated.

We are on sounder philosophical ground when we provide grants to those who are neediest. We should combine work and reimbursement for those who can be given jobs; and at the upper income levels of $40,000 to $60,000 we should continue to provide government-aided low-interest loans. Thus, there are issues beyond the nature of a form that need to be examined as we try to find the best ways to use public dollars.

SENATOR PACKWOOD: Under the Packwood-Moynihan bill, as it was introduced, 75 percent of the benefits go to people with incomes of $25,000 or less. And for the first two years of the operation of our bill, the maximum credit would be $250. The administration's bill, as introduced, gives a minimum grant of $250 to people with incomes up to $25,000. Thus, the terms of the two bills are very much the same. Furthermore, 75 percent of the beneficiaries of our bill earn less than $25,000, which is the case in the administration's bill. And, as Commissioner Boyer is aware, we have said to HEW that we are willing to negotiate and compromise.

There are only two bedrock principles that we insist upon: first, that the bill apply to primary and secondary education; second, that we use the tax credit approach. Short of that, we even went so far as to say we would be willing to combine the administration's approach and ours. Thus, if a student received a $250 grant, that grant would take the place of his tuition credit.

The administration turned us down flat. Yet, for 75 percent of the people who would be eligible under our bill, it would cost nothing, because the grant would offset a credit. The administration turned us down, not because of money, but because of philosophy.

MR. RYOR: There is a much wider problem that is being

avoided here. And that is the constitutional question whether or not the federal government has any responsibility to fund private choices. There are a variety of examples I could cite in support of my position on this matter.

For instance, if public recreation does not satisfy the needs of individuals, we establish private pools without any expectation that there will be a tax credit for those private pools.

If a company is not satisfied with police protection, it hires extra security, but without any expectation of tax credits paying for that special security.

Likewise, I think one could demonstrate that private roads and private property are built day after day without any expectation that there will be a tax credit or money from the public road funds to build them.

We have set out to make public education available, and to bring together in that setting people of diverse beliefs, backgrounds, religions, and cultures. We must get on with teaching children, not only to do the best they can under the circumstances or according to their abilities, but to appreciate all aspects of American society. That is not possible in separate and different educational systems that are based on religion.

PROFESSOR SOWELL: That is an interesting objection to making the Packwood-Moynihan bill a constitutional amendment, but its proponents have not chosen that approach.

Proponents of the bill have not said that people have a right to a separate, narrow education. They claim, rather, that the general public would benefit from this legislation, in the same way that the public benefited from the GI bill, which followed a similar approach. It was not assumed that people had a constitutional right to a GI bill; rather, the bill was considered wise public policy.

And concerning need, I should point out that there are

more people in nonpublic schools with incomes between $5,000 and $10,000 than there are people with incomes above $25,000. And there are more low-income people than there are people with incomes between $20,000 and $25,000. Thus, the concern about whether or not a few millionaires might benefit from the legislation seems inappropriate.

I think, too, that the costs of the legislation are greatly overstated. The figure $4.7 billion is often cited, but that figure represents Treasury disbursements. It does not give a true picture of costs in any meaningful economic sense.

In general, private schools are less costly than public schools, though private schools usually provide the better education. Many private schools spend half, or a third, sometimes only a fifth of the amount public schools spend. Thus, the real costs to society would be lower than the figures that are being tossed around.

Furthermore, we cannot predict the impact of the legislation by looking at the present distribution of people in public and private institutions. Clearly, the whole purpose of the bill is to provide opportunities for more people to have the kinds of education that only a few affluent people now have.

COMMISSIONER BOYER: I do not know what Professor Sowell's source of information is, but I disagree with his suggestion that public schools cost more. The legislation he favors also involves higher education where the average cost is $2,900 per year. The average cost of higher education in private institutions is about three times that.

My point is that we cannot look at the elementary and secondary part of this legislation separately. At least two-thirds of the Treasury loss would result from the tax benefit for higher education, if my statistics are correct. Therefore, we have to look at the costs at that level as well.

Further, I have to take issue with the suggestion that quality education is found only in the private sector. Is that supposed to be true at the elementary level or at the higher levels? UCLA is a public institution, and I would not judge it to be third rate.

PROFESSOR SOWELL: I was referring primarily to the elementary and secondary schools. Let me correct you about costs, though. You were talking about Treasury disbursements and tuition costs, which are not the true costs to society.

MR. RYOR: The question is absurd in any event. Throughout this country, many public schools are in bad trouble. We have a responsibility at the state and national levels to ensure that public education survives and is affordable. It must continue to provide to every child an opportunity to learn to the best of his ability. With the public schools in financial trouble, it is absurd to suggest that we should make available some system for bailing out and maintaining private education.

PROFESSOR SOWELL: I do not wish to bail out any kind of institution. We should make available to parents a choice, though. If enrollment at an institution rises or falls as a result of choice, we should allow that to happen.

MR. RYOR: The net effect would be the same. We would be using public funds to support private, parochial schools.

PROFESSOR SOWELL: Not necessarily parochial schools.

MR. RYOR: Most private schools are parochial.

SENATOR PACKWOOD: Are you objecting to public financing of private organizations? Or to income tax deductions that are allowed for supporting a private competitive agency?

Mr. Ryor: I object to using public funds to support private functions.

Professor Sowell: What about the GI bill?

Mr. Ryor: The GI bill provided money to adults, so that they could go to the colleges and universities of their choice.

Senator Packwood: Under our bill, the money goes to adults, too—for their children's primary and secondary education.

Mr. Ryor: The bill goes well beyond that. After 1980, these tax credits will increase in amount.

Senator Packwood: This debate about public versus private baffles me. Why is it considered almost immoral to allow a tax deduction for private competition with the public schools?

Look at the New York City hospital system. There is an immense municipal hospital system in New York, as well as a very good private hospital system. And we allow income tax deductions to support that competing private institution. Is there anything wrong with that?

Mr. Ryor: There is something wrong with supporting private education that is based on a religious point of view, or on an elitist point of view.

Commissioner Boyer: I would like to return to a point Professor Sowell made. We should not talk selectively about data that relate to the elementary, secondary, or higher levels. We should look at the whole spectrum.

It is my understanding that, under the Packwood-Moynihan bill, at least half of those eligible at the higher education level would be earning $25,000 or more. That is a high level of income. Senator Packwood is welcome to respond to that if my facts are incorrect.

Further, designing a public policy to provide tax relief for people at very high income levels, without recognizing their relative capacity to pay, cannot be taken lightly. At the level of higher education, we are talking about a sizable amount of money. It will cost billions of dollars to provide tax credits to people with incomes above $25,000.

PROFESSOR SOWELL: But you missed the point.

COMMISSIONER BOYER: I am sorry if I did, but I thought I was speaking directly to the issue.

SENATOR PACKWOOD: All right. I will make you a deal, Commissioner.

COMMISSIONER BOYER: Good. [Laughter.]

SENATOR PACKWOOD: If I put an upper limit of $25,000 on tax credits and guarantee that any grant will be offset against the credit so that people cannot have both, will you support it? Will the administration support it?

COMMISSIONER BOYER: We will not support it if it does not include the important combination of grants, work-study programs, and loans. The answer is to relate the resources we have to need.

SENATOR PACKWOOD: I was referring only to the grants. We will keep the work study and the loans.

If we put a $25,000 ceiling on credits, which is the Pell proposal's ceiling for grants, will the administration agree to it?

COMMISSIONER BOYER: I think not. We now have in place a program that provides almost full tuition credit up to an income level of $15,000. And we are proposing to extend that to $25,000. In effect, we have a descending scale of aid. Beyond $25,000, we ask the institution to provide work-study money, and we offer the high-income people a loan so that they may help their children through school.

SENATOR PACKWOOD: Let me make sure you understand the offer I am making, Commissioner. I am talking about just the grant, not the work-study program or the loan program. If somebody happens to get a grant for four or five hundred dollars, he cannot have any credit at all, because the amount of his grant is way beyond the amount of credit he is entitled to.

Will you give the student a choice between your grant program and our tuition tax credit program? It will not cost any more, because he cannot have both.

COMMISSIONER BOYER: As a practical matter, that would not be a reasonable trade-off. To allow choices and a combination of plans would create administrative complications. And it might not be worth the effort, since we now have in place a program that colleges and students are familiar with. I am not sure that we would gain anything from the alternative you pose.

SENATOR PACKWOOD: The alternative is this: We would need one line on the income tax form for the tax credit. If an individual has received any other grant that is in excess of the credit to which he is entitled, he gets no credit. Are you saying the administration regards that as an undue burden?

COMMISSIONER BOYER: It is an alternative I had not considered.

Senator Packwood: Are you aware of the approaches we have made to the Department of Health, Education, and Welfare on these compromises?

Commissioner Boyer: Yes, but I was addressing what I thought were the essential elements of the existing Packwood-Moynihan bill.

Senator Packwood: Well, can you speak for the administration as to whether or not it would accept this compromise offer?

Commissioner Boyer: Not at this moment.

Mr. Daly: I want to make one issue clear. When we speak about tax credits, we mean a direct reduction of the tax that is owed after all the other calculations have been made. It is not a deduction, but a credit.

Senator Packwood: For instance, if an individual owes $400 and has a $200 credit, he can take $200 off his taxes.

Mr. Daly: Let's discuss the possible impact of credits on public education. Would credits undermine support for public education, Professor Sowell?

Professor Sowell: Whenever people have a choice, there is no guarantee how they will exercise that choice. The main purpose of financing education should be to maximize the choice and the benefits of education, not to preserve whatever existing institution happens to be in place or whatever people happen to be benefiting from it.

The argument that has been used against the Packwood-Moynihan bill could have been used against the GI bill when it was first introduced. Only affluent people were going to college then, and the purpose of the GI bill was to change that. We have thrown around a lot of data based upon the existing distribution of people by income level, by religion, and so forth. One of the purposes of this bill is to make opportunities available to a much wider spectrum of people.

MR. DALY: Senator Moynihan has said that private schools lost a million students between 1965 and 1975, and that healthy competition between the private and public sectors in education is disappearing. Do you agree, Senator Packwood?

SENATOR PACKWOOD: Yes, I agree. Let's look at some percentages. In 1965, at the primary and secondary levels, 87 percent of the students went to public schools, 13 percent to private. Now, there are 91 percent in public schools and 9 percent in private, so there has been a 4 percentage point change in those years.

If, after its passage, our bill were to change the balance to 13 percent private enrollment and 87 percent public, the public schools would still have a very high percentage of students.

COMMISSIONER BOYER: This is an unhappy issue that is generated by the Packwood-Moynihan proposal. It tends to drive a wedge between public and private. I find that most unfortunate.

I want to remind Senator Packwood that our ends are the same. We are very much in favor of a strong private sector in education. We have a healthy tradition of diverse school systems, which we intend to support in all ways that are administratively and constitutionally appropriate. But we must do whatever is in keeping with good public strategy, and I believe that investing in a publicly supported network of schools is essential to this country.

Our society's first obligation is to see that public education is sustained, while in no way diminishing private education. And, of course, we must be constitutionally appropriate in what we do.

I cannot see why the argument of choice should be applied to the elementary and secondary schools and not to higher education. If we carry the argument to its limit, how can we defend tax support of the University of California? Why not go to a "tax credit" for higher education?

By what justification do we support the higher education system in California through taxes? We must ask ourselves if we really mean that the public, through its taxes and through its elected representatives, does not have the authority or the right to provide a system of general education that is in the interest of all, regardless of need. Public education is a centerpiece of our democratic society that must be preserved at all costs. It would be unfortunate if anyone viewed the defense of public education as a lack of sympathy to the rich and diverse private institutions.

As a matter of fact, in recent years there has been a resurgence of interest in private elementary education and higher education. In the state of New York, the enrollment trend in the past four or five years has been toward private colleges and universities. I think that is fine. It reflects choice, and the aid programs have allowed parents to make that choice. I hope we can affirm the public's traditional right to create a private educational program, while at the same time understanding the importance of the larger public sector.

PROFESSOR SOWELL: But let's remember that the working class, low-income, minority parent has one school that he can send his child to. And whether that child is taught or not taught, whether he is safe or not safe, he must go to that particular school.

The Packwood-Moynihan bill would extend a choice to the parent for the first time. Even if the choice is not exercised, the mere fact that the parent is enfranchised means that he must be taken seriously by the local bureaucrats, and that his child cannot be disregarded or disdained. Without choice, the child of a poor person is a captive audience. There is no reason for anyone to pay any attention to him.

MR. RYOR: I do not think that any child ought to be disdained or disregarded, or that his needs should not be met. Public education is basic to serving the diverse needs in this country.

There is no reason to support people who prefer their right of association to a free public education. Parents should not be denied the right to choose any school they please, of course, nor should their choice be interfered with by government. I do not think the government ought to subsidize that choice, though.

Free public education is the best hope for a free public society. If someone chooses a private education for his children, whether for religious training or for high academic standards, he should be the one who pays for it.

SENATOR PACKWOOD: Why just education, Mr. Ryor? Do we not allow tax deductions or tax credits to support private competitive noneducational institutions?

MR. RYOR: Earlier you mentioned the private and public hospitals. To my knowledge, the private hospitals are not advocating a particular religious point of view or trying to persuade their patients of a point of view. But that is not the case in most private, parochial education. Otherwise there would be no reason for those schools to exist.

SENATOR PACKWOOD: Let's separate private religious education from other private education for a moment. Would you be willing to allow the tax credit for the 20 percent of the primary and secondary schools that are not religious?

MR. RYOR: No, I do not think we should subsidize any private interest with public funds, regardless of the basis.

SENATOR PACKWOOD: In Bethesda, Maryland, we have a Bethesda-Chevy Chase Volunteer Rescue and Fire Department. It is a private organization, and I am allowed a tax deduction when I give to it. Do you disapprove of that?

MR. RYOR: That is a different matter. It does not involve the First Amendment question about religion.

SENATOR PACKWOOD: For the 20 percent of schools that are not religious, there is no First Amendment problem. Would you allow the tax credit for them?

MR. RYOR: No, I would not allow the tax credit unless the money was controlled by public agencies.

SENATOR PACKWOOD: There we are—it is really a question of control.

PROFESSOR SOWELL: I want to address this matter of religion. First of all, religious organizations conduct education for the same reasons that they establish hospitals, which are not "religious" hospitals in any real sense.

I have done some studies of black children in Catholic schools. It is not uncommon to find that three-quarters of the black children in a particular Catholic school are Protestants. And in one case that I know of, the principal was Jewish. [Laughter.]

What we are dealing with is a social service by a religious group. These schools serve an educational function for many people in ghettos. The Catholic schools, which were left behind when immigrant groups moved out, offer the only alternative to a public school education, which is very poor in many cases.

COMMISSIONER BOYER: May I clarify the issue before us for a moment? I thought we were discussing two alternatives—the Packwood-Moynihan bill and the administration's position.

I have heard so many concessions on the Packwood-Moynihan bill that I hardly know what we are talking about. We are now considering only 20 percent of the private schools.

SENATOR PACKWOOD: For point of argument, I suggested that we talk just about the 20 percent of schools that are nonreligious. I have no intention of giving up the other 80 percent.

Mr. Ryor raised the First Amendment problem, so I asked whether or not he would compromise on the 20 percent of schools that are nonreligious. But he was opposed to that as well.

Thus, he is not just concerned about the First Amendment problem. He does not want to support schools that the federal government does not control.

COMMISSIONER BOYER: We are supposed to be dealing here with two alternatives. The Packwood-Moynihan legislation, as proposed, does not contain the many exceptions that you mentioned, Senator.

If the legislation is passed in its present form, we calculate that it will make available far more federal aid to the nonpublic schools than is now made available to the children in the public sector.

That raises an important public policy question as to how limited resources should be awarded. Under limited budget constraints, it is hard to see how federal assistance to private schools can so far exceed what has been authorized for public schools on a per-pupil basis.

MR. DALY: Doesn't Senator Moynihan argue that we should take into account the federal deductions that are allowed for state and local taxes?

SENATOR PACKWOOD: That is right. Do you accept the tax expenditure theory—that money the federal government could tax but forgoes is, indeed, a federal expenditure, Commissioner?

COMMISSIONER BOYER: Yes.

SENATOR PACKWOOD: Well, if we count the real property tax and the state income or sales taxes that we are allowed to deduct from our income tax, and then look at the amount the federal government spends on education through those three tax expenditures, we can see that primary and secondary public education is being supported to the extent of about $5.8 billion a year.

Do you agree that those deductions are the same thing as expenditures in support of the public schools?

COMMISSIONER BOYER: Yes.

SENATOR PACKWOOD: The Packwood-Moynihan bill, in its full operation, will cost about $900 million a year in tax credits for primary and secondary private education. Surely you are not saying, Commissioner, that $900 million in tax credits to private schools is more than the federal government spends on public primary and secondary education in this country.

COMMISSIONER BOYER: I thought the bill was calculated to cost more than that when fully funded.

SENATOR PACKWOOD: Not for primary and secondary schools.

COMMISSIONER BOYER: Does the $900 million price tag include the tax exemptions provided to all private-sector institutions, including churches?

SENATOR PACKWOOD: No.

COMMISSIONER BOYER: Well, we must take everything into consideration in order to make a proper comparison. The evidence, based on our original estimates, suggests that the Packwood-Moynihan legislation would make the per-student aid to private schools higher than the aid to public schools.

PROFESSOR SOWELL: The point Commissioner Boyer has made about equity and income level constitutes an argument against the administration's bill. Given the fact that low-income people drop out of school at a high rate, any bill that concentrates the money at the college level (as the administration's bill does) is seriously biased against low-income people. And one reason such people never reach the college level is that they did not get the proper education at the elementary and secondary levels.

COMMISSIONER BOYER: We are doing more for elementary and secondary education, whether private or public, than you give us credit for, Professor Sowell. In at least ten different legislative authorizations, there is a mandate that some of the money administered by our office be provided to the nonpublic school children. We have worked out rather elaborate, and largely satisfactory, arrangements by which we provide materials, textbooks, and services that help to enrich the nonpublic school children. And a great deal of time and money is now going to public school children at the elementary and secondary levels because of the administration's determination to implement previous legislation.

PROFESSOR SOWELL: I am glad that much money and time are being spent, but if we neglect the matter of choice, the time and money will mean little.

MR. DALY: We must come to grips with two other areas in the time we have left. One argument is that tax credits to private education would foster racial segregation. Senator Packwood, do you consider this an issue?

SENATOR PACKWOOD: No institution—primary, secondary, vocational school or college—is eligible for the tax credits unless it qualifies under what is known as Section 501C(3) of the Internal Revenue Code. If it discriminates on the basis of race or anything else, it cannot get the exemption or the tax credit.

MR. DALY: Everybody agree to that? [Laughter.]
Attorney General Griffin Bell has declared that the Packwood-Moynihan bill is, on its face, unconstitutional. I doubt that we have the competence here to make constitutional judgments for the Supreme Court. The question we might discuss, though, is, Should the issue be allowed to come to a constitutional test, or should the attorney gen-

eral's statement be considered sufficient evidence that the matter should be dropped?

COMMISSIONER BOYER: No one could take the position that a given issue should not be allowed a court test. On the other hand, fairness to the public and prudence in making legislation are factors that must be weighed as well.

In a number of recent instances in the state of New York, legislation was passed which provided for rather open-ended aid to private schools. And time after time the legislation was judged unconstitutional. Thus, one cannot be casual about letting the courts decide. The courts should be called upon only after prudent action has been taken by the legislative and administrative branches. It is not in the public interest to act on a law, have one's name related to it, and vote for it, if there is serious question as to its constitutionality.

MR. DALY: Senator Moynihan has argued that if the case *Brown* v. *Board of Education* had not come before the Supreme Court and reversed *Plessy* v. *Ferguson,* our schools would still adhere to the principle of "separate but equal."

SENATOR PACKWOOD: And at the time the suit was brought on *Brown* v. *Board of Education,* many people in the administration said that we should not challenge the existing law.

Commissioner Boyer says we should look at this bill as a whole, rather than dividing it into its primary and secondary components. The bill *is* a whole. In the opening sentence of HEW Secretary Joe Califano's letter to Attorney General Griffin Bell, asking for an opinion regarding the constitutionality of S. 2142, the Packwood-Moynihan bill, he said to assume that the bill applies only to elementary and secondary education. Well, it doesn't apply only to elementary and secondary education. Since Califano suggested the answer that he wanted in that sentence, the opinion shouldn't carry much weight.

PROFESSOR SOWELL: Let me say something about another premise. We have been talking here about aiding institutions, but the bill is not written that way.

People do not favor this legislation because they want to aid institutions. They want to aid parents, and not only those who choose private schools, but also those who favor the public schools. The mere fact that people have the option to go to private schools changes the balance of power in a very critical way, and that is the very reason the education establishment objects to it.

SENATOR PACKWOOD: I might mention the last time I heard an administration make this argument. When Congress passed an act indicating that presidential papers belong to the public, the Nixon administration claimed the act was unconstitutional and had a Department of Justice opinion to back up that position.

COMMISSIONER BOYER: The constitutional issue was raised here secondarily, and I think rightly so. The issue before us should be discussed on more substantial administrative and public policy grounds. Yet, one cannot cavalierly suggest that it is not an issue to be weighed with the others.

SENATOR PACKWOOD: The bill's constitutionality is a valid issue, and honest doubts have been raised. But Senator Moynihan and I have taken the problem into account. Therefore, the provisions relating to primary and secondary education would not go into effect for two years. There would be an expedited court test at the start, before one dollar is ever spent.

MR. DALY: I think this would be a good time to let our friends in the audience open the question-and-answer session. May I have the first question, please?

LARRY SIBELMAN, American Federation of Teachers: My first question is addressed to Senator Packwood. Surely you recognize, Senator, that the government of the United States has a right to establish an armed force and that no one else does. It is clearly in the interest of the country to have a military that is governed by the President, and to allow no other army. And that relates to the question of democracy and public education, which is at the base of this debate.

Should not the public have an educational system that is preferentially treated by government agencies? Is it not fair to limit the financial support of institutions which are established essentially for interests of a private and exclusive nature?

Secondly, Senator Packwood is talking about some $4–5 billion going to private education through the tax credit. What will the costs be in another year or another ten years? Ultimately, will not this democratic institution be replaced by a fragmented series of private, parochial institutions that are designed to cater to particular interests of particular people?

MR. DALY: Senator, will you start?

SENATOR PACKWOOD: I think so. [Laughter.]
Let's look at the history of education in this country for a moment. No public schools as we know them existed until the 1820s in Delaware and until the 1840s in most other states. At the time the nation was founded, all schools that

educated primary and secondary children were church schools, and they received public money. Our forefathers thought nothing of appropriating public money to support these schools, even though they were sectarian schools that taught particular religions.

Does the country have a right to fund only public education? Certainly it has that right. And it has the right to give no benefit, no little tax break, to primary and secondary private education. But again, let's look at the figures. From the average taxpayer's standpoint, it doesn't matter whose hand is in his pocket. At present, state and local governments spend $61 billion every year for primary and secondary public education. And the federal government spends another $5–6 billion in tax expenditures. Against that, is it wrong to give a tax credit costing $900 million to private education? To me, $900 million versus $66 billion hardly represents unfair competition for the public school system.

Secondly, Mr. Sibelman asked what would happen to costs in years hence. I must answer that I have no idea. Certainly, expenditures for public education have increased in years past. But I hope that private education might be able to count on some public funds so that it can keep up with public education.

PROFESSOR SOWELL: Mr. Sibelman's assumption that there would be a proliferation of private schools suggests to me that people are very discontented with the public schools.

I cannot imagine why people would desert the public schools unless they were discontented. I also cannot imagine that the public schools would be unaware of what was happening as people who became enfranchised began to express their views. For instance, when blacks in the south became enfranchised, the white politicians discovered that blacks had last names and had titles and so forth. [Laughter.]

If the balance of power shifted, I believe that the public

schools would adjust and begin to take some interest in the students.

COMMISSIONER BOYER: In referring to earlier periods of our history, it should be noted that we did not educate everybody. We educated a select few, denying opportunities to most of the young people.

It was precisely in response to that narrow selectivity that we decided to make a network of public institutions available for all children, regardless of their social or economic status. And that is the central issue of our discussion here.

MR. RYOR: Moreover, I cannot believe that a $250 tax credit would influence significantly the poor parents' choice of a private school, when they would still be left with a large margin of tuition costs beyond that.

If there are problems in our public schools, it is important that we address ourselves to solving them. We should continue to put money in the local school districts where there are educational problems and special needs.

PROFESSOR SOWELL: We have put increasing amounts of money into those public schools. Mr. Ryor is suggesting that the money should be independent of performance.

Performance has gone down while the costs have gone up. According to the census of 1850, 59 percent of the free black people in this country were literate, even though they were forbidden to attend the public schools. So the notion that we must have a compulsory public school system in order to educate people strikes me as strange.

COMMISSIONER BOYER: I believe there is a direct relationship between the expansion of the public school system and the expansion of access. Our nation provided access to the elementary schools. Then we developed a secondary school system, primarily through the vision of Horace Mann and others.

And that opened up opportunities for higher education that had been denied to most of our young people for one hundred and fifty years. That cannot be casually dismissed; it must be reaffirmed as the public policy we are trying to sustain.

SENATOR PACKWOOD: Commissioner, Senator Moynihan and I have a record of giving overwhelming support to public education.

Neither of us has any intention of voting down the public school. Is the public school system threatened because 15 percent of the students might go to private schools, and because $1 billion (as opposed to $65 billion) might be allowed to support private education?

COMMISSIONER BOYER: I was speaking only to the suggestion that opportunity of access was not related to the development of a public school system.

PROFESSOR SOWELL: The opportunity of access may result from creating a public institution in the way that you mentioned, or from legislation like the GI bill, which gives the money to the individual and allows him to do what he likes with it. The crucial factor is money, not the particular institution through which it is filtered.

CRYSTAL KUYKENDALL, National School Boards Association: Professor Sowell talked about the notion of choice. I am concerned that the legislation he favors would not give lower-income minority parents a choice between private and public schools. What parent making $15,000 or less could afford the higher costs of private schools? If tuition tax credits went into effect, tuition for private schools would increase. What parent with five or six children would be able to afford the cost?

I have worked with numerous parent groups, and I know that the public schools need more support. I am concerned about the slur on public schools that I have heard here. What research findings show that school children who graduate from private institutions fare better in life than their public school counterparts?

My concern is not with GI bills or hospitals, but with education. It is important that we support our public institutions, because people who are disenchanted with them for reasons like desegregation will flee to the private institutions.

PROFESSOR SOWELL: As to how parents can afford private schools, I have found in my studies that tuitions are frequently between $350 and $400 a year for Catholic parochial schools in ghetto neighborhoods.

DR. KUYKENDALL: It's more like $1,000 to $1,200.

PROFESSOR SOWELL: No, that's too high. I have seen the schools. Some groups have been able to put together schools which cost far less per pupil than the public schools. The $250 or $500 tax credit would be more than enough at many of the parochial schools in ghetto neighborhoods.

As to how the students fare later in life, I have not seen a study about this. But I have seen studies reporting that the students are two or three years behind in some public schools that are spending $2,000 per pupil. In nearby private schools which are spending half or a third of that, the students are reading at or above the grade level. That is the kind of evidence that exists. The other evidence doesn't exist. If one wants to appeal to evidence that doesn't exist, one can, of course, maintain anything. [Laughter.]

MR. RYOR: In this country, we have dedicated a tremendous amount of time to integrating public schools and to making schools responsive to all of the citizens. Compare the number of children who are staying in school today to the number fifteen, twenty, or twenty-five years ago, at the time of the *Brown* decision. The schools have made magnificent progress in that area.

Professor Sowell cited statistics that private school children fare better than their public school counterparts. I don't know which private schools he was alluding to, but I suggest that there was probably a greater gap twenty-five years ago than exists today.

PROFESSOR SOWELL: But the public school pays $2,000 per pupil, and the pupils cannot read. In the same low-income neighborhood, children in the parochial school are reading much above that level for a lot less money.

COMMISSIONER BOYER: Choice is also related to location, and the access to private schools depends on whether or not there is a private school down the street. Otherwise one is limited to the high-cost residential schools. If we want true choice, it will be necessary to have equivalent options on the private level, and many of the so-called ghettos do not have access to private school options.

Not everyone has a real choice. Only occasionally is a private school convenient. Thus, I do not think the choice argument is a good one for changing policy.

PROFESSOR SOWELL: The same thing could have been said about the GI bill, that only some people could take advantage of it. But the whole purpose of the bill was to extend the option to attend college to more people.

COMMISSIONER BOYER: At the level of higher education, there is an assumption of mobility.

PROFESSOR SOWELL: But we have just been threatened with proliferation of the very schools that you say will be so scarce.

MR. DALY: Let's move on to the next question.

WALLACE SHERETZ, executive director, Education Association of Virginia: It seems to me that the bill is structured in such a way as to benefit the upper half of our society, to the detriment of the lower half. It is absurd to suggest that a low-income family given a $500 tax deduction will race out and send their children to a private institution. It is unlikely that they will be able to pay the remaining $1,500 in costs. It will take a lot more than the rhetoric that has been espoused here to convince me otherwise.

Professor Sowell, just what data support your contention that private schools are better, and that low-income people with a $500 credit can afford to send their children to better private schools?

PROFESSOR SOWELL: There are data to support the contention that most private schools do, in fact, have lower costs per pupil than do the public schools. And $500 is quite within the range of what will pay for education at this kind of institution.

In fact, there are people on welfare who send their children to those private parochial schools simply because the tuition is so low there.

MR. SHERETZ: Is the legislation designed for parochial schools then?

PROFESSOR SOWELL: Not at all. There are also Black Muslim

schools which operate without the frills common to public schools, and they manage to teach children to read and write.

Mr. Sheretz: So the legislation is designed for religious schools.

Professor Sowell: Not only for religious schools. The purpose of the legislation is to help people afford whatever kind of education they want, and to ensure that they are no longer a captive audience for the educational bureaucracy.

Barry Morris, associate superintendent, Fairfax County schools of Virginia: My question concerns the public schools, not the private.

Professor Sowell and some others have indicated that people are forced into an unhappy choice between inadequate public schools and no education at all. Yet, if we divert up to half of the federal support for education into private schools, how will we address the need of the so-called inadequate public schools?

Professor Sowell: If more money made schools adequate, the public schools would have been adequate long ago.

Mr. Morris: I would like Commissioner Boyer, too, to address this question as it relates to the bill that is supported by the administration.

Commissioner Boyer: I do not endorse the notion of diverting funds for reasons already discussed. Nor do I accept the idea that it is time to give up on the public system.

The record shows that our public education system has been remarkable compared with the systems of other countries. It would be a massive disservice to our national history and to the school teachers throughout this country to suggest that we have a failing system.

In some instances, our system has not been fully successful, but only because we have tried to do more than any other country. Moving children through twelve grades of education is, in my judgment, our greatest social accomplishment, and our scientific and economic achievements stand as a tribute to our educational system. It is our responsibility to see that the job of perfecting the public schools is completed.

ROBERT L. LAMBORN, Council for American Private Education: I am distressed by the division between the public and private schools, and by the assumption that two good systems are not better than one. I would like to affirm the position that having two good systems is healthy for American education and society. And I want to correct the statistics regarding socioeconomic background.

The most recent census figures show that, of families with children in private schools, 5 percent of the gross annual incomes are under $5,500; 10 percent are under $7,400; 25 percent are under $11,600; and 50 percent are under $17,100. These are hardly financially elite individuals.

Do the panel members see any option between the administration's grant program and the Packwood-Moynihan bill's tuition tax credit program which would serve the purposes espoused by both?

SENATOR PACKWOOD: Those of us who advocate tuition tax credits are willing to have a trade-off. People may choose the program they want. Since they cannot have both, the two programs will not cost any more than one.

So far, the administration has taken no interest in that approach, however.

COMMISSIONER BOYER: I like both the spirit and the openness of Mr. Lamborn's question. His reminder that both systems should have merit and support is the tone that should dominate.

It would be difficult to find the option you mentioned at the elementary and secondary level. Higher education seems to offer increased mobility, and I think some compromise plan might be reached at that level.

It is profoundly more complicated, though, to find an answer at the elementary and secondary levels. The administration's primary concern is that the current legislation be better administered.

We are committed to seeing that the authorizations in ten of our major pieces of legislation, which indicate that nonpublic school children are to receive services equal and equivalent to the public school children, are realized at the state and local levels. The constitutional problems among the states are rather complex, of course. But our present strategy is to see that 10 percent of the total authorization (which amounts to tens of millions of dollars) will be delivered to the private schools. That is the amount their enrollment would justify.

LAWRENCE ZAGLANICZNY, Coalition of Independent College and University Students: In the fall of 1975, 97 percent of the students in public higher education attended institutions that had tuitions and fees of less than $1,000. In private higher education, on the other hand, only 4 percent of the students were paying less than $1,000 in tuitions and fees.

The Packwood-Moynihan bill would cut the public sector's tuition bill in half by allowing everyone who is paying less than $1,000 to take off half of his tuition. Thus, the public-sector students would receive half tuition, whereas private-sector students would only receive 12.5 percent, if their tuition was $4,000.

Why does Senator Packwood hold to the conception that this bill is a benefit to private higher education when it clearly will upset the competitive balance between the two sectors?

Commissioner Boyer, do you think the Packwood-Moynihan bill, in its present form, will upset the balance?

SENATOR PACKWOOD: That is a very valid question.

Interestingly enough, the competition does not just exist between private and public universities. As a matter of fact, the public colleges think our legislation favors community colleges, because their tuition is lower than that of public colleges.

We had to make a decision as to how much we could spend, how much the public would accept, and how much the President would accept. We could have skewed the tuition toward a percentage of the total tuition, so that students at Dartmouth or Harvard would get roughly the same percentage as students at the University of Oregon or Portland State. But we decided on a flat tuition rather than a skewed tuition. It was simply a philosophical and financial decision that we made.

COMMISSIONER BOYER: The legislation does seem tilted toward the public, given the base of cost Mr. Zaglaniczny used.

In looking at the implications of competition, though, I would rather take into account the relationship of student need to the dollars made available. The tuition issue is secondary. Student need should be the criterion governing our use of money.

MARY GIREAU, office of Senator John Melcher of Montana: The Senate recently passed a GI bill that gave additional support to the Vietnam veterans. It gave the GI a flat amount of money for education. Surely we know what the result of this legislation will be. Every institution will raise its tuition. When an institution raises the tuition to $2,000, the GI will not be able to attend it.

Also, what about the vocational student? Everybody is worried about higher education, but I am worried about the fellow who might go to an auto mechanic school. He has to put money down for tuition that he would not get back until nine months later, so he can't go.

How can we answer those constituent concerns, Senator Packwood? In your bill, people are eligible for a credit only after they have gone to school.

SENATOR PACKWOOD: This is true for vocational schools as well as all others.

Ms. GIREAU: That's right, but how does your bill help such people?

SENATOR PACKWOOD: Let me first speak to the problem of institutions raising their tuition.

In three days of testimony about this issue on Capitol Hill, we did not find a scintilla of evidence that schools will automatically raise their tuition as a result of the tuition tax credit, or the GI bill, or the Basic Educational Opportunity Grant. Every school indicated that it did not wish to raise tuition.

Schools want to find other ways to cut costs, because they must compete for students. A study from San Francisco State indicated that there was no evidence of schools raising their tuition as a result of such legislation. People advance the argument, but do not provide a bit of evidence to back it up.

Our bill does apply to vocational scools. It applies to

part-time students as well as others. I will say again that, if the administration is willing to extend its grants program to all these vocational schools, we would be willing to give the student a choice. He could take the grant or the tuition credit but not both. The cost would be the same because one cancels out the other. Let's leave it to the recipient to decide. It is unfortunate that I cannot get any support from the administration for that position.

Ms. GIREAU: Well, Senator Melcher supports both bills. [Laughter.]

SENATOR PACKWOOD: You can probably find many congressmen who do.

PROFESSOR SOWELL: If the scenario that was just outlined is correct, it is hard to understand how so many millions of people were able to go to college under the GI bill who could not go before.

MR. DALY: Where there is a guarantee of funds, Senator, would it not be possible for the federal government to give an advance against the guarantee?

SENATOR PACKWOOD: It would be possible. I do not want to overestimate the likelihood of getting an advance, though. Again, I must come back to the position that we should allow the student a choice.

I was intrigued that a newspaper which had come out initially in favor of the Packwood-Moynihan bill later came out in favor of the President's bill. I asked the newspaper's board of editors why they had changed their minds. They responded that, after talking to a lot of people involved with the Basic Educational Opportunity and Work-Study Program, they had become convinced it was a better program.

Had they talked to any students? They had not. They had talked only to college administrators and people who were involved with HEW in the management of the program. Yet, it is interesting to note that, with few exceptions, the student-run college newspapers have come out on the side of the Packwood-Moynihan bill.

I don't know what the comparison signifies, but it is noteworthy that those who would be the recipients of our legislation seem to favor strongly the tax credit approach.

LEONARD DeFIORE, superintendent of Catholic schools, Archdiocese of Washington: Before I ask my question, I would like to present a few facts. In the archdiocese, the average tuition per child is $300. In the District of Columbia, we have about 10,000 children enrolled, 65 percent of whom are black, 30 percent of whom are non-Catholic. In terms of academic performance, our typical child in the class is learning at his grade level, not below.

As a public official, Commissioner Boyer, what does one say to parents who may be working two or three jobs in order to help their children to break the cycle of poverty? What does one say to the parents who find the public school in their neighborhood inadequate to their children's needs?

COMMISSIONER BOYER: That is a fair and thoughtful question. The fact is that the federal level provides no general aid to any school in this district. Our money is targeted to meet certain public purposes related to certain legislatively approved programs—education for the handicapped and for Title I children. We do not give general aid.

Therefore, at the present time, I do not see any way for the private school to receive general assistance, either directly or indirectly, beyond what has been determined as our proper federal role. If we do our job well, however, the children in the private schools who have the same kind of legislatively defined access to those programs should be served.

We have to avoid changing the present arrangement that requires federal money to be used to help children in pockets of great need, as defined by legislative mandate. I see no way to make an easy transition to general aid for the private schools. Yet, if we do the legislative job well, those children who have needs, as defined by law, should have access to federal services that have been approved by Congress. Thus, the private schools would be enriched secondarily.

PROFESSOR SOWELL: I notice that when we begin talking about parents, we immediately shift to talking about institutions.

COMMISSIONER BOYER: I did not mean to shift to institutions, except to say that the federal program cannot offer general aid to private institutions.

MR. RYOR: We tend to focus on the problem schools. We have about 16,000 school districts in this country serving kindergarten through twelfth grade, and probably as many divergent programs trying to serve a wide variety of needs.

If the schools do not serve the parents' needs, the parents have many mechanisms for change at their disposal. They can become part of the decision-making process that leads to the correction of inadequacies they perceive in the system.

We ought to encourage parents to take a greater role. By visiting the schools more often, and by expressing their viewpoints, they can become part of the policy-making process.

PROFESSOR SOWELL: If they had the right to take their business elsewhere, would they not have even greater influence?

Mr. Ryor: That right could pose a danger to the public schools. The parents' interest in quality public schools could diminish.

Professor Sowell: Is my influence as a consumer reduced when I have a choice of products? Do I have more influence over AT&T, a monopoly, than I have over smaller, more competitive companies?

Mr. Ryor: We have 16,000 school districts which are controlled by 16,000 different boards of education. Thus, I do not see what monopoly you are alluding to, Professor Sowell.

Professor Sowell: We have numerous phone companies, but for any given person living at any given location, there is only *one* phone company to deal with. That is largely what we have with the public school system.

Mr. Ryor: I still suggest that there are mechanisms for changing those public school systems and making them more responsive. Public funds and public participation are in the best interest of this country.

Tom Polgar, office of Senator Robert Morgan of North Carolina: It is an unfortunate fact of life that the most influential supporters of the public schools, whether through direct activity like membership in the PTA or indirect activity like political influence, are middle- and upper-income parents. And these are also the parents who support the Packwood-Moynihan bill.

If these people are encouraged to leave the public schools, won't efforts to improve the public schools be seriously undermined?

SENATOR PACKWOOD: I dispute your statement that only middle- and upper-income people support our legislation. Members of the Congress on Racial Equality testified very strongly in favor of the bill, and they are not normally thought of as representing upper middle-class whites. But they said the legislation would give them the chance for a competitive opportunity in downtown urban school systems.

Again I would reiterate that 9 percent of the people in this country go to private schools. If, by chance, the Packwood-Moynihan legislation changes that figure to 13 percent or 15 percent, the public schools are still not threatened. If it is seen as a threat that only 85 percent of the students go to public schools, then there must really be something wrong with the system.

MR. RYOR: Let us come back to the central issue. There is a question about constitutionality, which Senator Packwood claims to have made provision for testing at a later date. But the question of public aid to private schools has had at least sixteen court tests, three of which dealt with something similar to the tax credit proposal.

All of these previous decisions probably will not deter such proposals or settle the basic question, but there is plenty of court history to suggest that such proposals are not in the best interest of public policy.

PROFESSOR SOWELL: Regarding previous Supreme Court decisions, one of the key points was that the court did not want the federal government entangled with religious organizations, as would happen with direct aid to institutions.

Furthermore, the Supreme Court does not necessarily stay with one particular line of interpretation. In fact, some people in the legal profession have noticed a change in the court in recent years. Thus, I do not think we can assume that the legislation would not stand up to a court test.

BILL GRIBBIN, Senate Republican Policy Committee: We should not lose sight of the fact that we are here to discuss alternatives, not simply the Packwood-Moynihan legislation. Let us assume for the sake of argument, Commissioner, that the Packwood-Moynihan bill is bad educational policy and that it is politically inopportune.

There has been devastating evidence relating the recent tremendous increase in constant dollars for educational spending to the deplorable decline in student performance.

In light of that, Packwood-Moynihan misleads us; money has failed. How will we address the problem we are all concerned about—the cataclysmic decline in student performance at the elementary and secondary levels? What do you, Commissioner, suggest to our President as an answer to this hideous problem, besides more money?

COMMISSIONER BOYER: First, I do not accept the description of cataclysmic decline. I think we have become caught up in a very distorted and myopic description of the nature of our schools. In my view, we have gained much more than we have lost; we have excelled far more often than we have failed.

I am tempted, of course, to describe what I think might be the answers. They have to do with stressing language, and with making the secondary school a much more flexible institution, because students need to relate to work and collegiate experiences as they mature. And school should relate to the home because parents are the first teachers. We did not come here to discuss these issues, although I think they are more significant than funding alone. Again, it is a mistake to suggest that we have to choose between money and programmatic effort. It is the combination that will make our schools successful.

LORENZO MORRIS, Institute for the Study of Education Policy: My question concerns constitutionality and purpose. If we are to assure the liaison between the tax credit and education, then we have to make sure that the money from the tax credit goes to the indirect beneficiaries—the parents and students—and to the schools.

Evidence shows that there is an inverse correlation between family wealth and tax credit money used for education. But the question of constitutionality arises in the following way: If we are assuming that the tax credit has educational value, must we not state how the money is to be spent, what kind of schools people will go to, and how they are to be educated?

SENATOR PACKWOOD: If you are talking about supervision over the schools, I hope there will not be any. I hope there will be no more supervision than we have with the investment tax credit for business or the energy insulation credit that is in the energy bill. I do not want the kind of system that extends the tax credit only to people who will attend certain schools and meet certain criteria.

The greatest protection to our democracy is the diversity that existed at the time we started this country. It exists now. I would rather run the risk of a few fly-by-night schools than have a uniform federal policy, which would allow parents the privilege of collecting tax credits only if they send their children to certain described schools.

In its present form, the bill says that the parent and any accredited school can take advantage of the tax credit. I would not want to compromise that.

MR. DALY: This concludes another Public Policy Forum presented by the American Enterprise Institute for Public Policy Research. On behalf of AEI, our heartfelt thanks to the distinguished and expert panelists, Professor Sowell,

Senator Packwood, Commissioner Boyer, and Mr. Ryor, and to our guests and experts in the audience for their participation. [Applause.]